OUR STAR:
THE SUN

Contents

OUR STAR:
THE SUN

Barron's Educational Series

The Sun, the nearest star

The Sun is the central star of the Solar System. Planets move around the Sun attracted by the **gravitational force** of its huge mass.

In ancient time the belief was that the Sun was relatively small and was situated very near the Earth. Now we know it is much larger. Its radius is about a hundred times larger than that of the Earth and it is 93 million miles (150 million kilometers) from Earth, almost 400 times farther than the Moon.

The Sun is a star, that is, a huge ball of hot gas. Unlike all the other stars, the Sun is the only one near the Earth.

The next nearest star, Proxima Centauri, is 266,000 times farther away than the Sun. Consequently, we know more details about the Sun than about any other star.

Like most of the stars, the Sun's energy is created by transforming a part of its matter into energy by means of **nuclear fusion.**

In the reactions that are taking place inside the Sun, **hydrogen** is transformed into **helium.** The Sun loses four million tons of matter each second, but because of its huge size this loss is insignificant. During its life, which will last some 10 billion years, the Sun will lose less than 0.1% of its matter.

Below: Here you can see the planets in order outward from the Sun: Mercury, Venus, Earth, Mars, Jupiter, Saturn, Uranus, Neptune, and Pluto. Unlike the other planets, the distance between the Earth and the Sun provides the conditions necessary for life to develop.

CHARACTERISTICS OF THE SUN

Distance to the Earth: 93 million miles (150 million km) (12,000 times the Earth's diameter)

Diameter: 860,000 miles (1.39 million km) (109 times that of the Earth)

Temperature:
In the center: 59 million°F (15 million degrees°C)
On the surface: 11,000°F (6,000°C)

Period of rotation: approximately 27 days

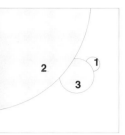

Below: The Sun ① is the central star of the Solar System. It is a star like the billions of stars in our galaxy. Nevertheless, because of its nearness to the Earth, ② the Sun is of vital importance to us. The Earth is a habitable place where living beings have been able to develop thanks to the energy radiated by the Sun. On the contrary, the Moon, ③ is too small to retain an atmosphere so no life has developed on it, though it is the same distance from the Sun as the Earth.

The formation of the Solar System

All of the Solar System, that is, the Sun, the planets, their satellites, and the rest of matter that forms the asteroids, the comets, the meteoroids, and the interplanetary dust, has the same origin.

The Sun, just like the rest of the stars, was formed from interstellar matter, present among the stars of our galaxy in the shape of gas and dust clouds.

About five billion years ago, a cloud of interstellar matter was condensed as it was going through a spiral arm of our galaxy. This started a chain of events in which the cloud started collapsing on itself because of its own weight.

The central part, which condensed because of the weight of the whole cloud, grew extremely hot. The rest of the cloud flattened and began to rotate. It formed a thin disk moving around that central object. When the temperature of the center reached several million degrees, the nuclear fusion of hydrogen began and the Sun began shining intensely.

Below, left: The planets that had just been formed suffered from an intense bombardment of meteorites.

Below: The Solar System (in the illustration outlined by the square) is found near the outer edge of our galaxy, the Milky Way. The middle is made up mainly of hydrogen. It also has measurable amounts of other chemical elements.

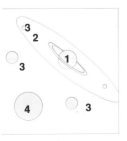

Below: The interstellar dust and gas that gave rise to our Solar System gradually fell toward the center where the Sun was formed ①. The rest of the matter began forming a disk ②, in which clusters developed and began to collide forming proto planets, the primitive planets ③. The growth of these heavenly bodies caused the planets to form ④. Their gravitational force attracted still more matter from the nebula which fell on them in the form of constant meteor showers.

The inner structure of the Sun

The Sun, like most of the stars, consists of a series of concentric layers of gas. The visible surface of the Sun is called the **photosphere** (sphere of light). It is not a solid surface. On the contrary, it is a thin layer of very rarefied gas.

The nuclear reactions that produce the Sun's energy are taking place just in its nucleus, that is, the extremely dense and hot central part of the Sun. The matter in the nucleus is so hot that it can support the whole weight of the star without being compressed. The energy is produced in the nucleus as **photons**, high energy light particles. Those photons are absorbed and emitted by the Sun's atoms many times as they make their way towards the surface. They gradually lose energy and, at the same time, they make the matter in the upper layers of the Sun hotter.

Near the surface of the Sun temperatures are very different from those in the deeper layers. This causes movement of all the matter, like the movements in a pot of boiling water. This phenomenon is called **convection**.

Over the solar photosphere, there is a layer called the chromosphere (sphere of color), only visible during a total solar eclipse. Farther out from the Sun, the chromosphere turns into the solar **corona**, a very hot area.

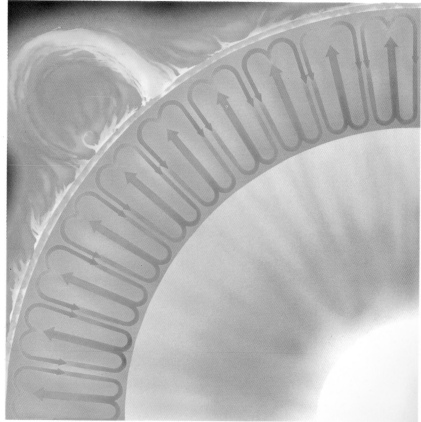

Left: During a total solar eclipse, the solar corona is visible. It extends a great distance from the Sun.

Below: The layers of the Sun under the photosphere are not very powerful heat conductors. Convection movements are produced during which the gas below grows hot, rises, cools, and falls down again.

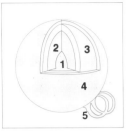

Below: The central nucleus of the Sun ①, where the nuclear reactions that produce solar energy are taking place, occupies up to one-fourth of the Sun's radius. Inside the Sun ②, the energy is transported towards the surface. Near the surface, convection movements ③ like those in a pot of boiling water, take place. Sunshine has its origin in the surface or photosphere ④. Over it, sometimes we can see large archlike prominences ⑤.

Sunlight

Sunlight is white. In fact, it is made up of light of many different colors. The spectrum of colors that make up sunlight can be seen, for instance, when a rainbow forms after a rain shower.

When the spectrum of sunlight is observed carefully with a suitable instrument, a large number of narrow lines can be seen. This means that in the large spectrum of sunlight there is more than one particular wavelength of light.

The visible light is just one possible form of **electromagnetic radiation**. Light with a wavelength shorter than violet light, which is not visible to our eyes, is called ultraviolet and is responsible for tanning us in the summer. On the opposite end of the spectrum of visible light is light with a wavelength longer than visible red light. It is called infrared, and we perceive it in the form of heat. This is the kind of radiation given off by an electric stove.

The Sun, though it produces most of its energy in the form of visible light, emits electromagnetic radiation of many wavelengths. The appearance of this energy at other wavelengths is quite different from what we know in visible light. For example, in X rays or radio waves, the Sun is not a uniform disk, but presents some surface areas with more intense emissions than in others.

Below: A rainbow appears when raindrops split up white sunlight into the spectrum showing its component colors.

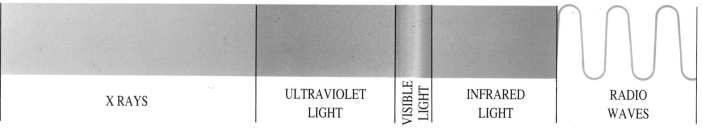

| X RAYS | ULTRAVIOLET LIGHT | VISIBLE LIGHT | INFRARED LIGHT | RADIO WAVES |

SPECTRUM OF ELECTROMAGNETIC RADIATION

Below: The Sun emits radiation in all the wavelengths of the electromagnetic spectrum. The appearance of the Sun in X rays is very different from the Sun in visible light. On the surface of the Sun, very bright areas ① that issue very intense X rays and very dark areas ② that do not emit X rays can be seen. X rays from the Sun do not reach Earth's surface because they are absorbed by Earth's atmosphere.

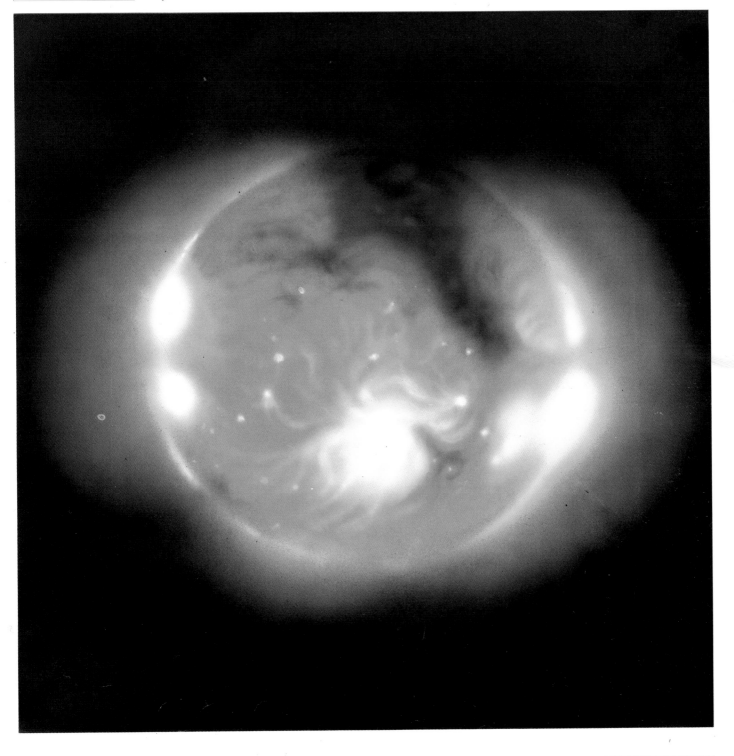

Observing the Sun

If the Sun's matter is so opaque, how can we gather information about what conditions are like in its center?

In the nuclear reactions that take place near the center of the Sun, **neutrinos** are produced together with high energy photons. The neutrino is a particle without an electric charge that moves at the speed of light. Ordinary matter is almost transparent to it. This means that the neutrinos produced in the center of the Sun can reach its surface in a fraction of a second, arrive at the Earth, and pass through it without a problem. Nevertheless, some "telescopes" have been built to observe solar neutrinos. Essentially, they are huge tanks, buried in deep mines to avoid any radiation other than neutrinos. The tanks contain a substance that is capable of capturing neutrinos.

Using this device, it is possible to measure the quantity of neutrinos produced by the Sun, which helps us to gain information about conditions inside the Sun. The measurements obtained by means of these solar neutrino detectors give rather surprising results. They have detected fewer neutrinos than expected from our knowledge about the Sun. The Sun, though it is the best known star, still holds many surprises.

Below: A solar neutrino detector is made up of a huge tank of liquid capable of capturing neutrinos. It is submerged in water and buried deep underground.

PROTECTING WATER

TANK

Below: All kinds of telescopes are used to look at the Sun. Most of them are installed on the Earth's surface. But, in order to look at radiation that does not pass through the Earth's atmosphere, telescopes have to be sent into space in rockets or in artificial satellites. The manned orbiting laboratory Skylab, shown in the illustration, had a solar telescope from which many observations of the Sun were made. Skylab was launched in May 1973, and remained in orbit until July 1979, when it entered the Earth's atmosphere and burned up over Australia.

Sun spots

When we project the image of the Sun on a screen with a small telescope, we usually see the solar surface marked with dark spots. These sun spots can be seen with the naked eye when they are unusually large. (*Beware! Looking directly at the Sun is dangerous! It can cause serious and permanent damage to your eyes, even loss of eyesight.*)

Sun spots are areas on the solar surface that, because of their contrast with the rest of the photoshere, have a dark appearance.

Sun spots allow easy observation of solar rotation. Every day a spot is displaced with respect to the previous day, as it follows a path parallel to the solar equator.

When a spot disappears on the west **limb** of the Sun, some days later, if it is intense enough, it appears again on the east limb. The rotation period of the Sun, seen from the Earth, lasts about 27 days.

The number of spots on the solar surface is not constant. It depends on a cycle of approximately eleven years. At the maximum point of the **cycle of solar activity** (the most recent maximum point was in 1989), there are always many spots on the Sun's surface. On the contrary, at its minimum, it is possible that no spots appear for many days.

Some of the maximums are very intense (for instance, that of 1957), whereas, occasionally, there are long periods when there are almost no sun spots at all. This type of minimum happened during the seventy year period between 1645 and 1717.

Below, left: Sun spots are not uniform. In every spot of this group, there is a darker central part and a shaded outer part, called the penumbra.

Below: Owing to the solar rotation, every day the spots appear displaced with respect to the previous day.

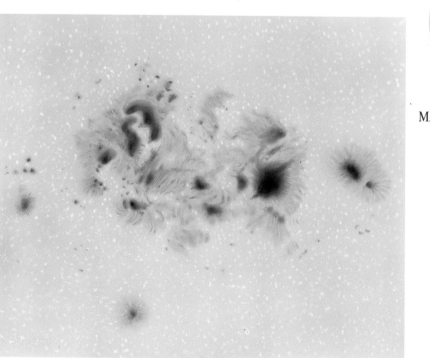

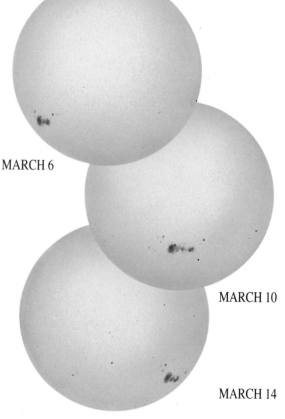

MARCH 6

MARCH 10

MARCH 14

Below: In the solar disk, there are usually small dark spots. They are called sun spots and are slightly colder, less bright areas than the rest of the solar surface. In sun spots, the magnetic field is especially intense, which causes the matter to be colder. While the normal temperature of the photosphere is about 11,000°F (6,000°C), the temperature in a sun spot is about 2,100 degrees cooler. Since it is cooler, the shine of a sun spot is much dimmer than the rest of the photosphere.

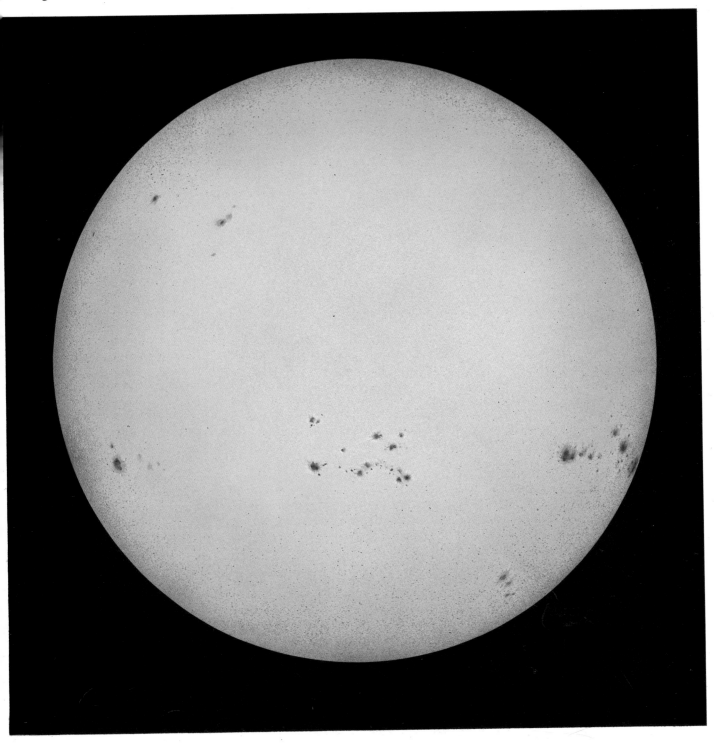

Solar flares

Sometimes, as during a total solar eclipse when the Moon completely hides the Sun, it is possible to see something similar to large red flares that emerge from the Sun's surface and extend beyond the Moon's limb. They are called *solar prominences*, or flares.

To study solar flares it is not necessary to wait for a solar eclipse. If the Sun is observed by means of a filter that lets in just the red light given off by hydrogen, the flares can be easily seen. This is the way they are observed.

Solar flares are clouds of hydrogen that normally appear at the bottom of the solar corona, having higher density than the rest of the corona matter. Flares are better observed on the Sun's edge. They can also be seen on the solar disk, but then they resemble dark filaments.

Some flares can be very large, reaching thousands of miles in length.

There are solar flares that last a long time, days and even weeks, while others come and go in a few hours.

The varying shapes of solar flares are caused by the magnetic field of the Sun, which causes matter to move in snake-like tracks, curling or forming flaming filaments.

The solar flares follow a cycle similar to that of sun spots.

Below, left: The solar flares often resemble flames because of the wave-like path the matter must travel compelled by the magnetic field of the Sun.

Below: Looping solar flares are the most spectacular seen on the Sun.

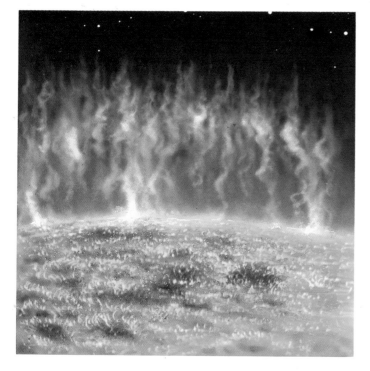

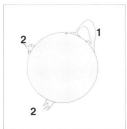

Below: Huge solar flares in the shape of arches ① and a flame ② rise above the Sun's limb. Solar flares are formed by hydrogen that condenses from the soft solar corona. They fall upon the Sun's surface following paths marked by the magnetic field of the Sun. Solar flares use a large amount of solar energy and are the most spectacular phenomena that can be seen on the Sun's surface.

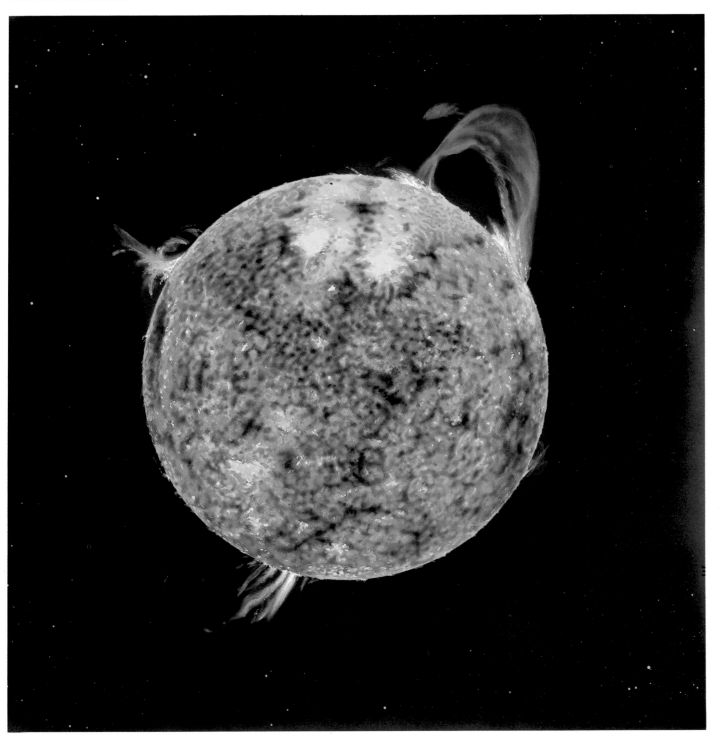

The solar corona

The Sun does not end abruptly at the photosphere. Above it, there is what we call solar atmosphere. At the bottom of this atmosphere, there is the chromosphere, which is a thin transitional layer between the photosphere and the high atmosphere. The corona is the outer part of the solar atmosphere. It is a thin, hot area that extends a great distance from the Sun.

To see the corona, it is ideal to wait for a total solar eclipse, when the Moon completely hides the solar photosphere. Then, a luminous halo can be seen around the Sun. It is usually quite flat, depending on the solar equator, and appears to rise from the Sun. This is the corona. Today, special telescopes are used to study the corona. In these telescopes the solar disk is hidden and some conditions similar to an eclipse are reproduced.

The temperature of the corona is extremely high; it can even exceed two million degrees. Since the corona is so hot, it emits part of its radiation in ultraviolet light and X rays. In spite of its high temperature, the quantity of energy contained in the corona and emitted in the form of light is very low, since the matter of the corona is thin and transparent.

The shape and extent of the corona also varies with the cycle of solar activity. During maximum solar activity, the corona has elongated extensions that reach out long distances.

Below: The corona can be studied using a special telescope called a corono-graph, that hides the light of the solar photosphere.

Below: The solar corona, which is very hot, intensely emits photons of high-energy X rays.

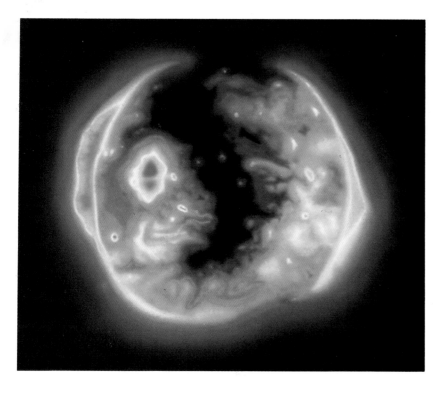

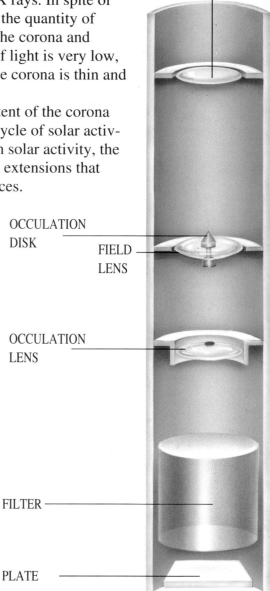

OBJECTIVE LENS

OCCULATION DISK

FIELD LENS

OCCULATION LENS

FILTER

PLATE

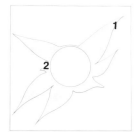

Below: During a total eclipse, when the Moon hides the light of the solar photosphere, the solar corona ① appears in all its splendor. Then, it is visible to the naked eye. Several solar flares ② can be seen near the solar limb. The shape and extent of the corona vary greatly during the eleven-year cycle of solar activity. At the maximum activity level, the corona can extend in elongated shapes to distances greater than the Sun's diameter.

The solar wind

The solar corona, the outer part of the solar atmosphere, does not end abruptly at any precise place. The temperature of the matter it is composed of is so high that the solar corona is always expanding. There is a continuous flux of matter that moves away from the Sun at high speed. This is the so-called solar wind.

The solar wind is made up of free **electrons** and hydrogen and helium **atoms** (the main components of the Sun) that have lost their electron shell.

The velocity of the solar wind is remarkable; about 250 miles (400 km) per second.

At this speed, the particles of the solar wind take four or five days to go through the interplanetary medium and reach the Earth.

The matter that forms the solar wind is extremely thin.

In the interplanetary space near the Earth, the solar wind contains only five particles per cubic centimeter. This is much less than the most perfect vacuums that can be produced in a laboratory on the Earth.

Consequently, the Sun is continuously losing matter as it produces solar wind.

The amount of matter that the Sun loses in this way is approximately a million tons per second. But the Sun is so large that this represents only the smallest fraction of its total mass, even if the solar wind goes on blowing with the same intensity for billions of years.

Left: In some comets, two tails can be seen: a straight and bluish one formed by gas, and a curved and yellowish one, formed by dust.

Below: Since the Sun is constantly spinning, the particles that form the solar wind move away in a spiral pattern.

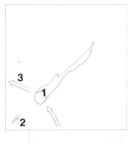

Below: The solar wind is a diffuse stream of matter, given off by the Sun at a high speed. Comets are affected by its existence. The gas and dust that evaporate from a comet because of the Sun's heat are pushed by the solar wind, causing the spectacular tail of the comet ①. Driven by the solar wind, the gas tail always points in the direction opposite the Sun ②, no matter what the movement and direction of the comet is ③.

Solar eclipses

The Moon moves along its orbit around the Earth passing between the Sun and Earth every month during the phase of the new moon. Usually, as we see it from the Earth, the Moon passes above or below the Sun. But, sometimes, the Moon passes exactly in front of the Sun, causing a solar eclipse. This usually happens two to four times every year. During a solar eclipse, the sunlight over a small area of the Earth is hidden by the Moon. For a short time, just minutes, night falls and the stars can be seen in the sky. Around the area where the total solar eclipse takes place, there is a large area where the Moon partially hides the Sun: this is where a partial solar eclipse takes place.

Another factor makes solar eclipses especially interesting. The Moon and the Sun, as we see them from the Earth, both appear to be the same size.

Actually, the Sun is much larger than the Moon, about 400 times as large, but it is also some 400 times farther away. These differences in size and distance cancel each other out.

TOTAL SOLAR ECLIPSES 1994–2000	
Date	**Areas where it will be visible**
Nov. 3, 1994	Central America, South America, Antarctic Circle, South Africa, Madagascar
Oct. 23–24, 1995	Somalia, Arabian Peninsula, Asia, Japan, Oceania, Australia
March 8, 1997	East Asia, The Philippines, Japan, NW of North America, Alaska
Feb. 26, 1998	Hawaii, Southern and Eastern North America, Central America, Northern South America, Caribbean Sea
Aug. 11, 1999	NE North America, Greenland, Arctic Circle, Iceland, Europe, Northern Africa, Arabian Peninsula, Asia

Below: The Moon completely hides the Sun in just a very small area of the Earth. In a larger area a partial eclipse takes place.

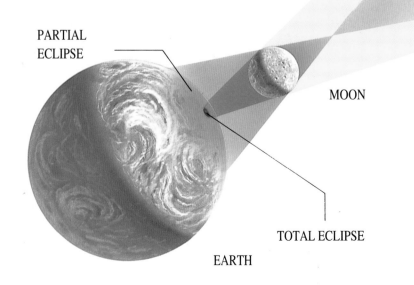

SUN

PARTIAL ECLIPSE

MOON

EARTH

TOTAL ECLIPSE

During an eclipse of the Sun, the Moon hides behind the solar photosphere by being between the Earth and the Sun. Since the intense light of the photosphere can't be seen, the outer and much softer, dimmer areas of the Sun become visible.

Below: The Moon and the Sun, when seen from the Earth, appear to be the same size. When the Moon is precisely between us and the Sun, a total solar eclipse takes place. At the central point of the eclipse, the Moon hides the light of the solar photo- sphere and the soft light of the solar corona is seen. In the smaller squares, you can see the different phases of the eclipse.

The Sun's influence on the Earth

The Sun, in addition to providing the light and heat necessary to make the Earth a habitable world, has other influences on our planet.

For example, the ultraviolet radiation from the Sun that reaches the higher altitudes of the Earth's atmosphere, at about 62 miles (100 km), detaches the electrons from the atoms and molecules of the air giving rise to a layer called the ionosphere. This layer reflects long-wave radio signals and allows radio communication over large distances between different continents.

Most of the Sun's ultraviolet radiation is absorbed in other lower layers of the atmosphere, at about 16 miles (25 km) high: the *ozone layer*.

Moreover, the Earth is not an isolated body in interplanetary space, but is bathed in a continuous wind of particles from the Sun. This causes a series of effects on the magnetic field of the Earth.

The magnetic field of the Earth that extends into interplanetary space is called the **magnetosphere.**

You may already know that iron filings on a sheet of paper placed on a magnet will align to the lines of magnetic force, from one pole to the other. The same thing happens to the charged particles of the solar wind when they enter the magnetosphere of the Earth. Many of these particles remain caught in two belts that go around the Earth, called **Van Allen Belts.**

Below: Approximately along the Earth's axis, there seems to be the equivalent of a large magnetic bar. The north magnetic pole of this bar is near the north geographic pole.

IONOSPHERE
MESOSPHERE
STRATOSPHERE
OZONE
TROPOSPHERE

Left: In the ionosphere, a long-wave radio signal broadcast, for example from Africa, bounces back to the ground and may be received in North America.

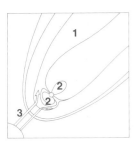

Below: The magnetic field of the Earth extends into interplanetary space, forming the Earth's magnetosphere ①. The Earth is surrounded by two areas called the Van Allen Belts ②. These contain the charged particles from the Sun ③ that are caught by the Earth's magnetic field. The Van Allen Belts were discovered by the first artificial satellites launched from the Earth.

The auroras

One of the most fascinating shows that can be seen in the night sky in high **latitude** areas are the auroras. Sometimes at night near the polar circles, a brilliant red and green gleam appears. The auroras adopt the shape of an undulating curtain, a flare, and sometimes, an arch. They usually cover a great deal of the sky. In northern areas they are also known as the "northern lights."

An aurora is caused by high energy particles given off by the Sun as the solar wind. Many of these particles are captured in the Earth's Van Allen Belts. If the number of particles that reach the Earth is very large, they can pass beyond the Van Allen Belts. They go along the lines of force of the Earth's magnetic field and enter the high atmosphere through the magnetic poles. At a height of 62 miles (100 km), the atoms of oxygen and nitrogen in the atmosphere are hit by these charged particles which separate some of the electrons from the electron shell. When they are reunited with the lost electrons, the atoms emit light of characteristically green and red wavelengths.

Auroras can appear near both poles. When near the north pole, it is called aurora borealis. If it takes place near the south pole, it is called aurora australis.

Below, left: Auroras are produced by high energy particles given off by the Sun. They reach the Earth's atmosphere through the polar areas along the lines of force of the Earth's magnetic field.

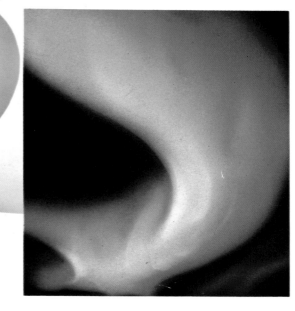

Below: An aurora that lights up the night sky in high latitude areas is a fascinating show. The atoms and molecules of the atmosphere produce the colored lights of the auroras. During the eleven-year cycle of solar activity when there is a maximum of sun spots, auroras can be seen more frequently. Sometimes auroras can be seen even at latitudes of 40° or lower, though they normally appear closer to the poles.

Activity: The colors of light

RED

ORANGE

YELLOW

GREEN

BLUE

VIOLET

**WAVELENGTHS OF
THE COLORS OF THE RAINBOW**

1 angstrom unit = 1 ten-billionth of a meter

Color	Angstrom Units
Red	7,000
Orange	6,000
Yellow	5,800
Green	5,100
Blue	4,700
Violet	4,000

Have you ever tried to break down the white light from the Sun into the spectrum of colors it is made up of?

Nature provides us naturally with the spectrum of sunlight. The rainbow that sometimes appears after a rain shower shows all the colors of sunlight. In the inner side of the rainbow, there is the color violet, and going outward we find the colors blue, green, yellow, orange, and red.

If you don't want to wait for a rainy day to see the rainbow, you can make one yourself with the help of a hose. Put your back to the Sun and spray water into the air. In front of you, you will be able to see the rainbow caused by the water drops.

If you want to study the colors of the spectrum of light more closely, you will need a glass prism. You can use any non-flat piece of glass. If you don't have any, you can get one at an optical supplier or toy store.

The best way to get a good spectrum of colors is in a sunlit room through the corner of a shade that shuts out light well. Darken the room and let a sunbeam in. Intercept the ray with the prism and reflect the rainbow you get on the wall or on a white sheet of paper.

This way, you will be able to see the colors of sunlight in detail. Notice the range of colors and how they change gradually from one end of the spectrum to the other.

Below: A prism can break down the white light from the Sun into its component colors. If you intercept a ray of light with a prism, you will get the spectrum of colors, from violet to red.

Right: It is easy to create a rainbow with the help of a hose. Put your back to the Sun and spray water in front of you. The rainbow will appear.

Glossary

atom: The smallest particle of matter. Atoms combine together to form molecules of substances.

convection: Movements of solar matter in a layer below the Sun's photosphere, similar to those in a pot of boiling water.

corona: The Sun's atomospheric layer, very thin and hot, above the photosphere.

cycle of solar activity: Cycle of eleven years during which sun spots and other phenomena associated with solar activity become less or more frequent.

electromagnetic radiation: Radiation that, depending on its wavelength, may be gamma radiation, X rays, ultraviolet radiation, visible light, infrared radiation, or radio waves.

electron: The main part of an atom, together with a proton and a neutron. Atoms can be distinguished by the number of electrons, protons, and neutrons that they have.

fusion: A nuclear reaction that is produced within the Sun, through which an enormous amount of energy is released. The reaction in the Sun is the union of four atoms of hydrogen to form one atom of helium.

gravitational force or **force of gravity:** The mutual attraction of the masses of two bodies, especially celestial bodies.

helium: The element that forms in the Sun's nucleus from hydrogen. A helium atom is made up of two protons, two neutrons, and two electrons.

hydrogen: This is the most basic of all the elements. A hydrogen atom is made up of a proton and an electron. The stars—among them our Sun—are three quarters hydrogen.

latitude: The angular distance, seen from the center of the Earth, between the equator and a point on the Earth's surface.

limb: In astronomy, the visible outline of a celestial body.

magnetosphere: The area around the Earth where Earth's magnetic field exists.

neutrino: A particle carrying no electric charge, with no mass, produced by nuclear reactions.

nuclear reaction: The joining of light atoms, such as hydrogen—in a *fusion* reaction, which takes place in the Sun—or the breaking down of a heavy atom, such as uranium—in a *fission* reaction, which takes place in nuclear powerstations. Enormous amounts of energy are created through nuclear reactions.

photon: Particle of light. The energy of photons is inversely proportional to the radiation wavelength. Thus, the most energetic photons are those of gamma radiation, and the least energetic ones, those of radio waves.

photosphere: The visible and bright surface of the Sun, from which sunlight comes.

Van Allen Belts: Areas around the Earth where charge particles (protons and electrons) from the solar wind accumulate.

Index

English translation © Copyright 1993 by Barron's
Educational Series, Inc.
The title of the Spanish Edition is *Nuestra Estrella:
El Sol*

© Copyright 1992 by Parramón Ediciones, S.A.
First Edition, April 1993
Published by Parramón Ediciones, S.A.,
Barcelona, Spain.

Author: Robert Estalella
Illustrator: Marcel Socías

All inquiries should be addressed to:
Barron's Educational Series, Inc.
250 Wireless Boulevard
Hauppuage, New York 11788

Boldface words are explained on page 30.

Library of Congress Catalog Card No. 93-18067

International Standard Book No. 0-8120-1739-0 (P)
0-8120-6370-8 (H)

Library of Congress Cataloging-in-Publication Data
Available on request.

PRINTED IN SPAIN
3456   98765432